HELLO STRANGER

A Full Length Play

by Sharon Yablon

Hello Stranger was first produced by Theatre of NOTE in Los Angeles, CA, Fall 2017. The production was directed by Sarah Figoten Wilson. The cast and crew were as follows:

Audrey: Aliyah Conley and Maren O'Sullivan
Mike: Trevor H. Olsen (alternate cast Jonathon Lamer)
Carla: Reamy Hall (alternate cast Nicole Gabriella Scipione)
Mandy: Elinor Gunn (alternate cast Jennifer Flack)
Carpy: Christopher Neiman (alternate cast Brad C. Light)
Jesus: Alexis DeLaRosa (alternate cast Isaac Cruz)

Produced by David Bickford, John Colella, Reamy Hall, John Money, Kirsten Vangsness
Stage Manager: Kelly Egan
Lighting Design: Martha Carter
Set Design: Fred Kinney
Props Designer: Michael O'Hara
Sound Design: Marc Antonio Pritchett
Costume Design: Kathryn Wilson

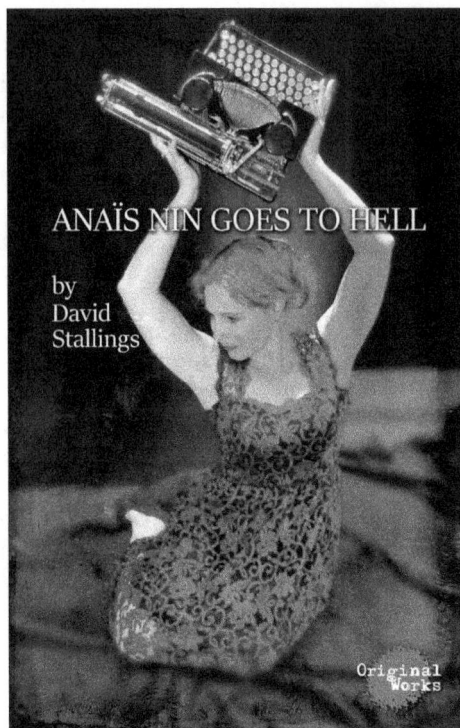
2

CHARACTERS

AUDREY - A young girl who teeters on innocence and a maturity that is muted and never precocious. She is barefoot and wears a top and shorts, with a boomerang clasped in them. She has an ethereal quality.

MIKE – Old enough to have baggage. A combo of gruff and gentle, a sort of likable loser. He is haunted by his past in ways he might not consciously realize. He wears a suit that's a little disheveled, with a blue flower on it.

CARLA – early 40s, white trash but that is just her exterior. She is cautious and her anger hides a deep sadness.

MANDY – 30s, flirty, with a sense of lost 1940s glamour. She is on a road to self-destruction. Her moods are changeable, and she has bouts of confusion which can unsettle her.

JESUS - A lewd mariachi of mysterious origin. His costume is thrown together from regional flora and fauna, dirty feathers, bells - a piñata of a person, or a scarecrow. He can be creepy at times in that he knows things, like a fairy tale character.

CARPY – Wily and nomadic like a cowboy, and although he buys into the lifestyle, he grapples with loneliness that's underneath any "edge" he presents. He's a mixed bag of having committed minor crimes but with a heart that feels things and regrets.

THE SETTING is a mixture of a dream and real version of Fontana and the Inland Empire, whose rural life and open space is rapidly being developed. There is still a sense of history there, going back to the Indians and early settlements, and a lurking danger that you might not find in cities. Its past charms are buried under scuz. The time is late October, and Halloween and The Day of the Dead Festival are its backdrop.

THE SET is a red and gold panel painted on the back wall to depict a sunset. Bits of a fence that has unraveled are along the back wall. A tree with scant leaves is in the corner. Some leaves may be on the stage.

THE SONGS mentioned in stage directions were used as inspiration in the writing process, story, and character. They are an obscure mix of 50s doo wop, 60s, ballads, and lounge. Licensees are solely responsible for obtaining formal written permission from copyright owners to use copyrighted songs in the performance of this play and are strongly cautioned to do so. Licensees are solely responsible and liable for all song clearances and shall indemnify the copyright owners of this play and their licensing company and agent, Original Works Publishing, against all costs, expenses, losses and liabilities that may arise from song us-age.

HELLO STRANGER

PART ONE

Scene 1

(A sound cue starts off as disconnected party sounds with some 80s music that is mentioned in the play, which blends into rural nighttime outdoor sounds, which blends into fiesta music, which blends into female humming of Frank Sinatra's "In The Wee Small Hours of the Morning." Humming starts off more expansive/echoing and becomes simpler and representative of a child as lights go up. When they go up, it is clear that Audrey is now singing and the echoed quality is gone. She is near the tree. Mike enters and watches her from afar. Some blood runs down his temple and he is a little disheveled. Audrey stops humming.)

MIKE: Don't stop.

(She stares at him.)

MIKE: Was that a Justin Bieber song?

(She shakes her head no.)

MIKE: I guess you don't have Bieber fever.

(Pause.)

MIKE: I fell asleep in my car. Woke up, rolled down the window, there was distant fiesta music. And I thought, a person could just stay here, exist in their car. They don't need the world. . .my great grandfather came out here looking for gold. Know what he found?

(She shakes her head no.)

MIKE: Syphilis, from a hooker who betrayed him.

AUDREY: Is there any gold left?

(He comes more onto the stage.)

MIKE: Sure!

AUDREY: Where?

MIKE: In the pits. You can follow tracks the carts used to take miners down underground. It's darker than dark. What's your name?

AUDREY: What's yours?

MIKE: Mike. I hope I don't scare you. Do I? It's just I heard your singing. And I followed it.

AUDREY: Followed it?

MIKE: Like it was a sweet road. And it led me here.

(She stares back at him.)

MIKE: Last night I went to my 30-year high school reunion. That probably seems like a long time to you. Well you're right, it is. They were playing Kansas, Haircut 100. Music from when I was young. The room swirled, did I tell you I was drunk? There were pictures on the wall, of all the people who had died from our class. You don't know this, but some of the kids from your class will die soon.

AUDREY: Sherman died.

MIKE: See what I mean?

AUDREY: He was riding his dirt bike. The desert is over there.

(She looks off.)

MIKE: Do you go into the desert?

AUDREY: We get date shakes.

MIKE: Yum. Ever see anyone in uniform out there?

AUDREY: Like a dentist?

MIKE: Why'd you say that?

AUDREY: I don't like them.

MIKE: I don't like them either. But no. Like a marine. Sometimes they go to war and come back. Stay away from them.

AUDREY: I'll hit them with my boomerang.

(She unbuckles a boomerang from her belt, ready to throw it at him.)

MIKE: I'll behave then.

(He bends down near her.)

MIKE: These your dying tomatoes?

AUDREY: They're Carla's. She kills stuff.

(Pause.)

MIKE: Reunions are weird. Even though you knew these people before, there's nothing to say to them now. There was this woman there. She looked half attractive, the way people do at parties. I guess I lived with her the summer after high school. She tried to remind me of our apartment in Hollywood. Some orange cat. But I didn't remember.

AUDREY: Why?

(Her question throws him for a beat.)

MIKE: I felt like a shmuck.

AUDREY: What's that?

MIKE: A dirt bag. But, I shouldn't have gone. I'm embarrassed about my life. Everyone has a house, kids. Do I look like I don't know how to get those things?

(Audrey shrugs.)

MIKE: Becky's gone; I couldn't even make that work. I planned a trip to White Sands for us. In the middle of nowhere I held Becky. It's always been over, I told her. The sun was a fireball and we made love. I let her be on top because I didn't want to do any of the work. This fine sand was all in and up my ass for days. It's still there. Reunions. Nothing of value is communicated. And then it was 4 AM. I went outside. Somebody had taken animal tranquilizer. It was somewhere between night and day, and a pimp came towards me. Fontana. You like living here? Marooned, out on the 10?

(Pause, she looks at him.)

AUDREY: I think you went to that party expecting something. If those people didn't like you then, they won't like you now. I guess you could stay in your car, like you said. Drive around. Park. People will know about you.

(She wanders, looks out.)

AUDREY: There's orange trees here, from when the groves were great. The smell is part of the air, but so is hog shit and truck exhaust. I like it here because I'm here.

(She ends up at the stage edge, sits, looks up. He joins her and looks up too; there is a quiet sense of not knowing who or where they are or how big the universe is. Carla is seen peeking in.)

MIKE: Our star's gonna die someday.

AUDREY: What will happen to us?

MIKE: We'll burn. But I like space anyway.

AUDREY: Yeah.

MIKE: I heard an astronaut talk about it once. He said seeing Earth from the moon was the most beautiful thing he ever saw. And being away from it was the most crushing loneliness he ever felt.

Scene 2

(Carla enters. She holds a rolling pin. She addresses Mike.)

CARLA: Stand up!

(He does.)

CARLA: Don't move!

(He doesn't.)

CARLA: Step away from her.

(He takes a step.)

CARLA: Who the fuck are you?

AUDREY: He lives in his car.

CARLA: What?!

MIKE: That was just an idea.

CARLA: You better start making sense.

MIKE: My car hit something. I think.

CARLA: Is that my problem? Are you hurt?

MIKE: I've got a hangover. Parties are hard. I want to talk to people but I'm not smooth so I drink.

CARLA: Where's your car?

MIKE: Just out there, ma'am.

CARLA: Don't call me that, I hate that.

MIKE: What should I call you?

CARLA: You shouldn't call me anything.

AUDREY: That's Carla.

MIKE: Oh, Carla.

CARLA: What, you know me?

MIKE: I've heard things.

(He smiles at Audrey.)

CARLA: What did you hit?

MIKE: I'm not sure.

CARLA: People don't fix their dogs and cats here.

MIKE: I saw a drum of something, rolling.

CARLA: They dump toxic stuff out here. They're killing us all and they don't care.

MIKE: No, it's okay.

(There's something tender in his voice and it almost comforts her but she's protective.)

MIKE: I heard your daughter singing.

(Carla and Audrey look at each other, a secret between them.)

MIKE: The sound traveled over the freeway, through downtown Fontana and the thugs and porn shops. Teens selling themselves along Sierra Parkway.

CARLA: What's so great about where you live?

MIKE: LA? Not much.

CARLA: LA's got problems.

MIKE: I know.

CARLA: I spent some time there.

MIKE: Were you trying to be an actress?

(She looks at him, annoyed.)

MIKE: You're better off, they're all nuts.

(He breathes in the air, looks out.)

MIKE: Sunsets are prettier out here. The smog enhances the light.

CARLA: No it doesn't.

MIKE: I grew up here.

CARLA: Good for you.

MIKE: One of my friends had horses. We'd go into the hills, ride them around, like the Indians. I haven't been back in a long time.

(He stares off. Something in her slightly softens and she doesn't like it.)

CARLA: You can't just go into someone's yard.

MIKE: Okay.

CARLA: I need to make my daughter dinner.

MIKE: I wish I had a daughter. I've gotten a few women pregnant and they've all chosen to abort. Some have even said, I'm definitely aborting this. Is it something about me?

CARLA: Look. I can give some food to you. But you have to stay outside.

(He stares back at her.)

CARLA: Fried chicken and salad. And that's it. Then back to LA. Or wherever. It's not my problem.

MIKE: Okay.

(Lights change to reflect sunset. They all look out. Sound of distant dogs barking.)

MIKE: Rabid dogs. I remember that sound. They answer each other. It's kind of beautiful.

CARLA: No it's not. They're strays and they have babies. They're out there in a world that someone else made. The mothers troll around, with the pups holding onto their nipples, their little bodies dragging across the asphalt. They sleep in alleys or the holes in someone's foundation. I heard a lot

18

of them live in the sewer, and that could be. They get shot, people like their guns out here. They get driven over by a dirt bike, people like their dirt bikes out here. Sometimes other dogs kill the mother and eat the pups. Or the homeless eat them. They're born so small, it's so easy.

(Carla has a quiet sadness. Audrey takes her hand.)

AUDREY: Meth heads hide their stash up their butts. They forget about it because their brains are fried. When the baggies open all of their veins pop and they die in a burst of blood.

CARLA: I'm going to close the sliding glass door and lock it.

MIKE: I would.

(Carla and Audrey turn to exit. Audrey breaks away and hands Mike a napkin.)

AUDREY: You got blood on you.

(Mike wipes his forehead as Carla watches, before lights fade and she exits.)

Scene 3

(Bug zapper sound, intermittently throughout. Lights up on Mike, he sits on a cheap lounge chair. The purple light of the zapper glows in the back. He eats from a paper plate as Carla watches, nearby. Audrey is near the tree. He finishes.)

CARLA: There's no dessert.

(Audrey wanders out. SOUND OF AN ICE CREAM TRUCK.)

AUDREY: Ice cream!

CARLA: I don't want any.

MIKE: You don't need to worry, you have a nice figure. No one wants a Karen Carpenter whose heart will stop in bed.

(Carla is annoyed but also doesn't mind his flirting. Audrey notes their interaction and exits.)

MIKE: I think it's been awhile since I've eaten. Thank you.

(Carla doesn't answer.)

MIKE: I forgot how nice it is here at night. No heli-copters. Or screams from Satanic blood cults. I live in Hollywood.

CARLA: I figured.

MIKE: But I'm not a star.

CARLA: That's too bad.

MIKE: Fame has eluded me.

CARLA: I wouldn't want it.

(He stands, faces her.)

MIKE: Wouldn't you? Isn't it a sort of love?

(He looks out.)

MIKE: A Playboy bunny lived in the apartment next to me. She was from the 50s, around the time the magazine launched. She was old now. One day she had a massive stroke. No one knew and she started to mummify. I noticed mail sticking out her front door. I managed to get in the apartment and there were these pictures around of a beautiful young woman on magazine covers, out on the town. I followed the putrid scent to a body. It was lying on a bed on a pink bedspread, with some letters around. I read one. It was from a fan of "The Attack of the 50 Foot Woman." I didn't know who I was living next to until she was dead. I didn't know she was alone.

(Pause, telling this has an effect on him.)

CARLA: I loved those Creature Feature movies. They scared me. But I would rather watch them then be with my shitty family.

(She feels self-conscious that she revealed something about herself.)

MIKE: Does she have a father?

CARLA: It's none of your business.

MIKE: I was just curious.

CARLA: Well don't be.

MIKE: You can ask me a question.

CARLA: I prefer a cigarette.

(She lights one.)

MIKE: My grandparents came over on a boat.

CARLA: Whose didn't.

MIKE: I'm a Taurus. You like astrology?

CARLA: We're not on a date.

MIKE: That's good. I don't think I'm doing very well.

Scene 4

(Audrey enters with an ice cream bar, she gives it to Mike.)

MIKE: Look at that.

(He takes a bite, relishes it.)

MIKE: Peppermint stick, with the bits of candy in it! I haven't tasted this in about 40 years! I used to get it at the Woolworth's.

CARLA: That's gone.

(He is surprised, saddened.)

MIKE: Why?

CARLA: What do you mean why? Next you're going to ask about the drive-in.

(He looks at her questioningly.)

CARLA: It's a Quiznos now.

MIKE: The soda fountain was my favorite spot. Eating your sundae in those tall glasses with the scalloped edges. Sitting on a stool at the counter, your feet dangling. It was like the despair of the world couldn't ever get you in there.

(Audrey wanders towards the stage edge. She looks back at Mike and as she does lights shimmer near her, like the reflection of a pool. He seems to recognize something and is drawn to it.)

MIKE: There was a pool here. . .

(He moves towards her. A strange mood has come over him. He wavers a little.)

CARLA: You have to go.

(He falls, passed out.)

CARLA: Shit.

(Lee Hazelwood's "Wind, Sky, Sea and Sand" plays. Audrey goes to Mike and kneels at his side. She holds her hand elevated over his stomach. She begins to make slow circles over him with her hand, a child's odd gesture but also indicative of something deeper, mysterious. Carla watches, and then looks out. She takes a drag from her cigarette, lost in her own thoughts. Slow fade.)

PART TWO

Scene 5

(Lights up. Mike is still laying on the ground. A liquor cart is in the corner; bug zapper and lounge chair are gone. Mandy is onstage. She wears a peignoir, plum lipstick, and her shoulder length hair has a 1940s wave. She stands in profile with a cigarette and takes a long drag, letting the smoke ooze out of her mouth like a Vargas pinup. Blackout/lights up. Mandy's cigarette is gone. She looks out as if concerned about something. Blackout/lights up. Mandy now looks down at Mike. He comes to, slowly stands, a little confused as song ends.)

MANDY: Hello stranger.

MIKE: Hi.

MANDY: Have you seen my son?

MIKE: I don't know who he is.

(Disappointed, she turns away.)

MANDY: Downtown is that way. The desert is that way. The artists are that way, in Idyllwild. If you like bad art. Well, you're a looker, aren't you?

MIKE: I don't know about that.

MANDY: Rugged.

MIKE: If you say so.

MANDY: Want a drink?

MIKE: No.

MANDY: Oh, that won't stick.

MIKE: Yeah, I've tried it before.

MANDY: Can you stay? Just to talk, because I have
    a reputation.

MIKE: I haven't heard anything.

MANDY: I like sex.

MIKE: That's good.

MANDY: People say I give it away.

MIKE: That's bad.

MANDY: It's a small town and I could use some
    company. Too much darkness. I long for hands on

me, the whir of bodies. To escape. . .Halloween is so sad now. There used to be children.

(She turns to him, concerned.)

MANDY: What's happened to them?

MIKE: I don't know.

MANDY: The mothers are waiting. . .

MIKE: They almost always don't find the child.

MANDY: Are you a cop?

MIKE: No.

MANDY: I don't mind cops.

MIKE: I do.

MANDY: Their job isn't easy.

MIKE: Neither is a slaughterhouse worker's.

MANDY: I like "Harry-O," you remember that show?

MIKE: Didn't he live on a boat?

(She smiles coyly at him.)

MANDY: Not married?

MIKE: Two years is the longest relationship I ever seem to have.

MANDY: You need to work on that.

MIKE: I don't know how.

MANDY: You'll end up alone then.

MIKE: I figured I'd hook up with someone at my reunion.

MANDY: Reunion?

MIKE: High school.

MANDY: How did it go?

MIKE: It wasn't in the cards.

MANDY: There's always tonight. . .why don't you get me a drink? My father liked that liquor cart so much he often took it to bed with him.

MIKE: What do you want?

MANDY: You'll figure it out.

(She watches him make a drink and approaches, standing behind him.)

MANDY: But don't think about getting lucky.

MIKE: I won't.

MANDY: Because alcohol puts me in a warm bath of love.

MIKE: Sounds nice.

(He turns around and is surprised to find her there.)

MANDY: My male friends can hardly keep their hands off me.

(Beat. She touches him. The touch makes them both uncomfortable although this is unexpected. Nonetheless, she feels rejected. She tastes her drink.)

MANDY: A Black Russian. My favorite.

MIKE: I guess it's my specialty.

(He seems surprised by this. Something has shifted in the scene for them. She wanders toward the audience, looks out.)

MANDY: The mountains are dark. You just moved in next door?

MIKE: No, I live in LA.

MANDY: They keep putting takeout menus on the door even if somebody's dead inside.

MIKE: I don't think they care.

MANDY: The realtors stopped coming around. People hear things, about a house. It keeps things - memories, bad ju-ju, something like that.

MIKE: They tore down Sharon Tate's house because of the Manson murders. But Trent Reznor moved in first.

MANDY: Who's that?

MIKE: A rock star.

MANDY: He didn't mind the murders?

MIKE: I think they were inspiration.

MANDY: Don't you have a lot of murders in LA?

MIKE: Yeah, serial killers like palm trees.

MANDY: And all those poor starlets in garden apartments, crying, slicing their wrists. Could you live somewhere with a bad history?

MIKE: If it was all I could afford. I've been there.

MANDY: Where?

MIKE: Having to live, do things I didn't want to. I've lived in bad neighborhoods.

MANDY: Can't they change?

MIKE: Some do. But some remain the rotting shitholes they are.

MANDY: Why don't you make yourself a drink?

MIKE: As I said.

MANDY: Yes, on the wagon. But why don't you come off. . .for a pretty lady?

(He makes himself a drink. She clinks his glass. He finishes the drink, she follows.)

MANDY: You know I could have shot you, wandering in like you did.

MIKE: I don't remember wandering.

MANDY: I don't remember you wandering either.

MIKE: And we're not even drunk yet.

(She smiles at him.)

MANDY: Fontana was a lovely little town when we
moved here. So much charm.

MIKE: I heard the small town in America is disap-
pearing.

MANDY: Where's it going?

MIKE: I don't know.

MANDY: This house even had a white picket fence.

MIKE: That doesn't mean anything.

MANDY: Why not?

MIKE: Fucked up things can happen inside a cute
house.

MANDY: I was a girl when we drove out from the
Midwest.

MIKE: From where?

MANDY: Why, you know it?

MIKE: Not really.

MANDY: Just being polite, then?

(A beat of eye contact, and she faces the audience.)

MANDY: My father drove us out from Tulsa. There's a lot of Art Deco there, glittering and green. . .we drove in a station wagon. In Nebraska my father wanted to stop and run through the corn. My mother was annoyed with this playful side of him, his wandering mind, lack of ambition. She stayed in the car but I went with him even though I was scared; the corn was tall, and there were noises in it. We got the hell out of there. Then there were cows everywhere. It was a long drive and apparently I wasn't a very good passenger so I was given a valium. Drugged, I dreamt of milky worlds. When I awoke there were buttes and drifters. We picked one up, my mother was so mad. But my father was sweet, trusting. I loved him.
(The mention of him connects her to old pain.)
The drifter had long black hair, no bag or anything. He was exotic, an Indian, but I didn't really

understand that then. That we had killed them all. He sat next to me in the back. "In the Wee Small Hours of the Morning" was playing in the tape deck, it was my father's favorite. Do you like Sinatra?

MIKE: Sure.

MANDY: *(sings softly)* In the wee small hours of the morning, you'd be hers if only she would call. In the wee small hours of the morning, that's the time you miss her most of all. . .

(Her song has a weird effect on him, which persists for the rest of the scene.)

MANDY: I could smell the earth on the hitchhiker. He put his hand on my shorts; I watched its fingers creep under the lavender fabric. I could feel it become slippery down there, nobody had touched me in this way before. A knife glinted from his inside pocket. If I said something, cried out, maybe the Indian would hurt us. So I let him keep touching and he did, ever so softly, exploring. It felt good but I was trembling. After a bit he took his hand away. He wanted to get out. Where? My father asked him. Where the mountain meets the sky, he said. That sounds nice, where is that? He pointed, and my father stopped the car. The Indian got out. But I didn't want him to go. We drove away and I watched him from the back window. He smiled at me with crooked lips, dark eyes. (pause) At the time I thought it was my virginity that he took. It wasn't, but he took something. We got to California. To Los Angeles. But that didn't work out. And we came to the Inland Empire.

(She stares off, her mood has darkened.)

MANDY: I don't want to talk anymore. You found your way in. Now get out.

("I Apologize" by Sunny and the Sunliners plays. He watches as she stares out for a beat and finishes her drink. Then she walks the periphery of the stage back to the liquor cart. She puts her empty glass on it. She wheels the cart away, exiting. Audrey appears across the stage. She holds a red candle in a jar. She goes to Mike. She hands him the candle. She has vibrant face make-up on, that resembles a skeleton with flowers. She leads him to the edge of the stage. They look out as song finishes.)

Scene 6

MIKE: You're all dressed up.

AUDREY: It's the Day of the Dead.

MIKE: They have that on Olvera Street.

AUDREY: You like the first stand, with the taquitos and the avocado green sauce.

MIKE: Those are great taquitos.

AUDREY: And then you have a margarita or two. You watch the people and go home.

(She gestures.)

AUDREY: Recognize that?

MIKE: It's my car.

AUDREY: Not anymore. You leave something out here and it's not yours anymore.

MIKE: It's been spray painted. What is that? *(tries to look closer)*

AUDREY: The devil and a duck.

MIKE: They're walking into clouds.

AUDREY: Let's not go over there.

(Mike looks around.)

MIKE: There weren't houses here. It was a field with chaparral, and these purple wildflowers.

AUDREY: Only this is left now.

MIKE: Goddamn developers.

AUDREY: Everyone says that.

MIKE: Doesn't it bother you? Your home is changing?

AUDREY: Can't do anything about it.

MIKE: I used to come here. I liked the open land, looking for things. I found an arrowhead. And something else. *(trying to remember something.)*

AUDREY: There was a path down the garden, a secret way I walked to school. A man used to talk to me. He said he lived all alone in that Victorian house over there.

(She stares off, Mike looks.)

MIKE: That's a big house for one person.

AUDREY: That's what I thought.

MIKE: Something's not right about that story.

AUDREY: That's what I thought.

MIKE: But you didn't go see it, did you? He asked
  you to, didn't he?

(She doesn't answer. He gets stern.)

MIKE: We could hurt you. And no one will give a
  shit about your boomerang. Do you understand?!

*(She runs off as he looks after her. Lights darken.
Sound of wind.)*

Scene 7

(Wind fades, lights brighten. Jesus is crumpled in the corner, a sombrero covers his face. Two goblets are turned over next to him. Carla enters with a bouquet of purple wildflowers. Mike watches as she places them down.)

MIKE: People leave flowers on the road in LA after a crash. Off Mulholland Drive you can see cars in trees from when they went over the cliff. They look like sleeping birds from a machine age.

(Pause.)

MIKE: My mother is buried somewhere. I haven't been to her grave. But what's the point, right? This is for us, not the dead. You feel better now, right? Because you left those flowers? But whoever that is, is still dead.

(Upset, she hits him. Toni Fisher's "The Big Hurt" plays. Jesus pops up.)

JESUS: Lovers, look at the two of you.

CARLA: We're not lovers.

JESUS: Aren't you tired of diddling your clitty alone on the couch with a beer? *(pause)* There's a taco truck over there, I suggest you get a few carnitas, enjoy them, they give you some potent gas so careful. Then fuck each other's brains out! And don't neglect around back, the woman needs to be shown that the anal is carnal! I just got out of the hospital, a back scratcher up my ass and she still didn't find the prostate!

MIKE: It's well protected up there.

JESUS: Yes it is! But the genitals are the most fragile. I dream of the days when my dick worked; now it's like a banana slug in my hands, bloated, yellow. They dump drums of toxic waste where I live. I get depressed about it, but Quaaludes help.

MIKE: I used to take those and listen to Led Zeppelin III.

JESUS: *(sings "The Immigrant Song")* Ahh! Ahh! We come from the land of the ice and snow, from the midnight sun where the hot springs blow! *(stops singing)* I get my ludes from the video store on Walnut Ave., you go past the roped off pornos and my god! The things that are going on in that back room!

CARLA: I've seen you.

(Pause, Carla and Jesus have a beat of eye contact.)

JESUS: And I've seen you, Senora. I have a periscope and I've seen those titties.

CARLA: You play over there with your son, near the tree. He can't catch or throw a ball.

JESUS: He's retarded. I don't like the term 'special needs,' there's nothing special about it. It sucks and his brain is a blob.

CARLA: You have so much patience. I want to tell you that it's beautiful.

(Pause; Jesus is moved by this but tries to hide it.)

JESUS: He knows nothing of his ego, and he loves unconditionally, what we all want but few can do. A great love was unearthed inside me when he was born. You know what I'm talking about.

(That has some significance for Carla.)

JESUS: I love the messiness of his emotions. The way he looks at the world, sweet and drooling. That fucking kid is curious about everything, where most of us could give a shit. He'll be a child forever, full of wonder. *(pause)* But he will need a woman, a hooker with daddy issues or mental mania, who will do anything, and won't mind my diseased ganglia as well. We have a beautiful life in the hills with other Mexicans. There are fresh tortillas. Wild chickens running around. Places to hike and dream.

CARLA: Where is his mother?

JESUS: We met when we were 11. I impregnated her immediately in the old Kaiser Steel Mill. *(pause)* He killed her coming out. And I hated him for a bit. But I'm not angry anymore. It doesn't get you anywhere. Every year we celebrate her at the Day of the Dead Festival. I tell my son about her, the shadow of her long eyelashes on the ground. *(pause)* I know you and we have never spoken and that's not right. My name is Jesus and I live in the hills of your town with my retarded son. We are deformed from the chemicals.

CARLA: I'm Carla.

JESUS: So, you guys burying a guinea pig here or some shit?

MIKE: Is there an actual cemetery around?

43

JESUS: People bury shit in this field. There's dead gang bangers, meth heads. ATV accidents. A lot of dead people in the Inland Empire. McDonalds hides their factory accidents here. Better check that order of French fries for a finger! I've got a few dozen hamsters around here, one of them my boy strangled.

CARLA: *(to Mike)* I can take you there.

JESUS: Oh no, get those carnitas and fuck! Listen to me missy, before your vagina dries up and retreats in shame with all the other old vaginas! And don't think they talk to each other. They are alone. Well, I'm off to an illegal truck stop. It's a beautiful place. There is no violence, just marijuana and strippers. They use a fuel rod as a pole. Some are horrid to touch, but I can assure you, everyone gets fucked.

CARLA: I hope to meet your son one day.

JESUS: His name is Luis and I have told him about the joys of the pussy and the a-hole. Are you busy later?

CARLA: I'm not going to have sex with your son.

JESUS: I'm sorry, I can't help myself.

MIKE: Couldn't you introduce him to other retarded girls? Maybe they'd fall in love.

JESUS: Yes, that is down the line, but I want him to have good sex first.

(Carla steps out and gestures.)

CARLA: The cemetery is over there.

(Mike joins her. They both look out. Jesus starts to back away.)

CARLA: At the edge of town.

(Jesus ends up back at the wall and slumps, covering his face with the sombrero.)

Scene 8

CARLA: Is your father buried there too?

MIKE: She told me he was a preacher. That he lost his mind in scripture.

CARLA: There are people like that.

MIKE: Then she said he was a fisherman. He left us for the sea.

CARLA: You never knew who he was?

(Pause.)

MIKE: One day a termite man came over, and he didn't leave for a few weeks. He was kind, he cooked us steaks. He danced with my mother to Fred Astaire and Ginger Rogers. And they drank. Finally, he had to get back to his wife. The walls to our house disintegrated, he wasn't a good termite man. A coyote came in. You could see stars where our ceiling fell. She liked that. *(pause)* There are pictures in my mind of her, but I don't know if they're real. She comes to me in dreams.

CARLA: There was a woman who used to live around here. She would wander through town in these dresses, like the kind in old movies. A ghost from another time, people thought she was a freak. But I wished I could tell her that no one wore hats and gloves anymore and it was good she was doing that, so we wouldn't forget how people used to be. There was talk. Of fathers bringing their sons to lose their virginity. Sad men whose wives had died of cancer. Old men trying to forget their futility. They all went to see her.

MIKE: My mother was the town whore.

(Pause, Carla takes this in.)

CARLA: I'm sure she helped a lot of people.

(Sound of distant children's laughter/celebration, but with an ominous undertone. Carla is drawn out.)

CARLA: The children! They've come back!

(She exits, toward the sound.)

Scene 9

(Jesus awakens. He hands a drink to Mike.)

MIKE: This is good.

JESUS: It's sangria from the slums of Hemet.

MIKE: I've been thinking about your son.

JESUS: Thank god for booze.

MIKE: What kind of life he'll have.

JESUS: It'll suck.

MIKE: Couldn't he surprise you?

JESUS: Like one night without stomach acid? I don't think so. The moments between us are so violently beautiful and then they are gone and I am breathless. I hope you have exhausted your woman and she lay in your bed, swollen and dreaming. I don't get invited much to dinner parties. I sour the conversation with reality. No one wants to hear anything bad, you know? Our parents are old and dying, and then we will be old and die, what should we do? My body is changing, getting uglier. Hairier. Viagra gives me an erection till dawn. It's pul-

48

sating, conjured by demons. Who will touch it, in the fire light?

(Yells to the offstage.) Throw the ball back, you fool! Aiyee, this is so hard! A shrink said to let the children be, to not always save my son from shame so he can feel life.

MIKE: He is looking up at the sky.

JESUS: God I love him.

MIKE: How can we know what he is thinking? He could be dreaming of terraforming new worlds.

(Pause.)

JESUS: There was a killer here. A killer of children. He lived in a house hidden by orange groves. It smelled sweet, but he wasn't.

MIKE: What happened to the killer?

JESUS: He got what he had coming.

MIKE: What was that?

JESUS: What do you think? The town got together. We stormed into the field, to his house. We ripped him apart.

MIKE: I understand.

JESUS: The parents here are grotesque creatures who have outlived their children. This goes against nature, like meeting a woman hornier than you. But there is a calm in this town now. The most terrible thing has already happened to many people here. Unlike others, in LA. They're scared, waiting for the horrors that will be but haven't taken shape yet. Come and watch the fuckin' sunset with me.

JESUS: But don't even try to jiggle my balls. Don't get any romantic ideas.

MIKE: It's strange not to feel the planet turning around. It's moving so fast.

JESUS: If gravity went away, we would all fall off in different directions. How do you die if you never crash into something?

MIKE: You suffocate in space. But you keep falling. And you become a skeleton twirling in the sky.

(Pause.)

JESUS: Don't drink all that drink now, okay?

(Jesus winks at him.)

PART THREE

Scene 10

("Hot Dreams" by Timbre Timbre plays. Mandy enters, dressed like a stripper. She approaches the audience and looks out, as if she is looking in a mirror. She checks her appearance. Pause; she starts to cry. Jesus hands her a pill from somewhere on his costume. He exits. She takes the pill. He re-enters holding a fuel rod, and stands stage center, extending it as lights change to red and blue, slowly flashing and turning, like a strip club. The drug she took takes effect, her mood changes. She starts to dance sultrily around the fuel rod as if it is a stripper's pole. She touches Jesus as a stripper would, and he plays the role but knows it is just that. After a bit Mandy sees Mike and she freezes; they stare at each other. A lot of feelings for both are under this. She approaches him slowly as song peters out, lights shift, and Jesus exits and re-enters with the liquor cart, putting it where it was before. Jesus exits.)

MANDY: Did you do your homework?

MIKE: I hope so.

MANDY: You're a good boy.

MIKE: I don't like school. I'd rather be with you.

MANDY: No, you should be with friends.

MIKE: I don't think they're around anymore.

MANDY: *(confused)* What time is it?

MIKE: *(looks at his watch)* Four o'clock.

(She turns to him, hugs him suddenly.)

MANDY: I've missed you so much! Where have you been?

MIKE: I don't know.

MANDY: I guess I overslept! But you got to school alright?

(Pause.)

MANDY: I'll get us dinner, okay, baby?

(She goes to exit, then stops. She is not feeling well. Mike goes to her, staying behind her.)

MIKE: Momma?

(He extends his drink to her. She turns around. Beat, she takes it, drinking it all.)

MIKE: I'm sorry it's not the dark drink.

MANDY: Oh, it doesn't matter! It's like when I give you Hi-C or chocolate milk, they're both good, right?

MIKE: Uh huh.

MANDY: So don't worry, okay?

MIKE: Okay.

MANDY: What is this, anyway?

MIKE: It's from Mexicans. Is it going to make you better?

MANDY: I'm already better. What should we have for dinner?

MIKE: I can call for a pizza.

MANDY: Don't we have that a lot?

MIKE: I like pizza.

MANDY: Me too.

MIKE: I don't like it where you work.

MANDY: It's fine.

MIKE: They look at you like they want to eat you.

MANDY: You're never to go there! I told you!
    (Tries to calm herself.) At night. Some people are
    awake and they can't sleep. They're scared and I
    just help them. Okay?

(He doesn't answer. She looks at him guiltily.)

MANDY: Shouldn't you be in Little League or some-
    thing?

MIKE: There are houses where the field used to be.

MANDY: Are the children cruel to you? I'll talk to
    the parents.

MIKE: Don't.

MANDY: Why not?

MIKE: The other mothers don't like you.

MANDY: Oh.

MIKE: Because of the dads.

(Pause.)

MANDY: Don't be mad at them. They're sad, sweet women who can't satisfy their men, understand?

MIKE: No.

(She looks carefully at him.)

MANDY: Your black eye has cleared up. I have a friend who's going to show you how to fight.

MIKE: The school bully has gone missing.

MANDY: Good, he was a creep!

MIKE: And others too.

MANDY: What is happening?

MIKE: Nobody knows.

MANDY: I worry about you.

MIKE: I think I'll be okay.

(She touches his cheek. Carpy's voice from offstage is heard.)

CARPY: Mandy! Get that sweet little ass back in here!

(She is conflicted.)

MANDY: He doesn't mean anything by that.

MIKE: Yes he does.

MANDY: Answer the door for the pizza man, okay?

MIKE: The pizza man has his own key.

MANDY: He's a nice man.

MIKE: Is the man in your room nice?

MANDY: Sure.

(She goes to exit. Lights change to evoke moonlight, she looks out.)

MANDY: The moon is right there, watching over you.

MIKE: Is it going to fall into us someday?

MANDY: If it does, you won't even feel it.

(She looks down at him and hugs him. She exits.)

MIKE: Gophers need the moon to see. So do ghosts. I saw a ghost but nobody believes me. Some people want to see them. They form groups and call themselves paranormal enthusiasts. But what would happen if they really saw one? I think they'd shit in their pants.

Scene 11

(Lights darken. Carpy creeps in. Mike has some trepidation about him. Carpy pretends to be in a shootout with Mike.)

CARPY: You know if this was the Old West, one of us would already be dead.

(A weird growl is heard from far off.)

CARPY: Chupacabra's coming.

MIKE: Those aren't real.

CARPY: Oh, they sure are.

MIKE: It is possible that in ancient times the legendary cryptid terrorized the Inland Empire.

CARPY: Show off.

(Pause.)

CARPY: So, you the man of the house? Name's John Carpy, but you can call me Carpy. Everyone does.

(Carpy holds out his hand to shake Mike's, they shake.

CARPY: Kinda little to be a proper protector, wouldn't you say? There was this kid. He was in all the smart classes and he had those big dumb glasses. In school I wouldn't be caught dead talking to a putz like him. But time passes. I wish I could take back all the times I broke his nose, but I can't. He did my homework for me, but he shouldn't have because I didn't amount to anything. So is my failure his fault? I don't know. Listen. There are things I genuinely feel bad about. A cat I outgrew 'cause he got old. And people, along the way. There's a woman in there. But you knew that already. If I wasn't mistaken, I'd say she was your mother. And that's your first problem. Well. I'll be going. And what happened in there. . .you'll see, when you get older. You almost never see eye to eye with a woman. And they're crazy. But it doesn't matter because they're so sweet. Now who else lives here?

MIKE: A cat.

CARPY: Yeah, I saw a scrawny orange bastard lingering in the hall. Anyone else around?

MIKE: No.

CARPY: I had a weird uncle who lived with us. Know what he did? I can't talk about it. It's too painful. Maybe when you get older. Maybe over a beer.

(Carpy steps away, looks out. Mike is curious about him, joins him.)

CARPY: I'm so alone. I get the feeling you know all about that. Get a horse. Build a fire. You can always survive out there. Remember that. It's our land. You and me.

MIKE: It was the Indians.

CARPY: They tell you that fancy shit in bullshit school?

MIKE: Yes.

CARPY: Big wow.

MIKE: I have an arrowhead.

CARPY: Yeah?

MIKE: And I saw petroglyphs too.

CARPY: How's that?

MIKE: Cave drawings.

CARPY: I'll be.

MIKE: It's mostly of them hunting. And some animals that aren't around anymore.

CARPY: Like a t-rex?

MIKE: No, Man couldn't survive amongst the great lizards.

CARPY: Any naked Pocahontases?

MIKE: I don't know.

CARPY: Ever seen a naked Pocahontas?

MIKE: No.

CARPY: Not even in a magazine? Well don't look at me kid! You don't got a dad to show you this shit? Did he die of a heart attack or something right in front of you? Dads seem to do that.

(Pause, this reminds Carpy of a bad memory.)

CARPY: Well where is he all this time? Gone fishin' *(laughs)*? I wonder if he knows he has a son, then. Feels it in his body when he's out in the world.

MIKE: I talk to him sometimes. When I'm riding my bike. Or at night when I look out my window.

CARPY: What do you see when you look out there?

MIKE: A line of lights where the houses stop. And then dark. What do you see out your window?

CARPY: An alley and a chicken leg. If your pop can't hear you, does it matter? Maybe it does, maybe it doesn't. Who am I to say? If anyone asks, the pizza man was here. Later, alligator.

("2,000 Light Years from Home" by The Stones starts. Carpy tips his hat.)

CARPY: In a while, crocodile.

(Carpy exits. Beat. Mike mimics a cowboy shootout, firing where Carpy exited. Then he looks towards the offstage, where Mandy's room is.)

MIKE: Momma? The pizza man was here, and I killed him.

(Beat. Mike goes toward the offstage.)

MIKE: Momma?

(Pause. Music builds. He takes a tentative step into the offstage. Blackout.)

Scene 12

(Song plays in the dark for a bit. Lights up - they are psychedelic and swirl around, eventually mimicking the lights from the pool as before. Mandy is in the center of those lights, as if she is "appearing" in them. Mike is nearby, observing this.)

MANDY: It's a glorious night!

(She turns to him.)

MANDY: Why didn't you come get me?

MIKE: I thought there was a man there.

MANDY: They go out my window. They never stay… what should we do? How about I teach you to swim?

(She beckons to him, he joins her. Her hand reaches out to him from the pool lights.)

MIKE: I don't like the drain.

MANDY: It just goes to another world.

MIKE: What's there?

MANDY: Trash and cakes. Hairballs and clowns.

(Something troubles her.)

MANDY: Where am I?

MIKE: Here.

MANDY: What day is it?

MIKE: It's today.

MANDY: No… what have I done?!

MIKE: You taught me to swim.

MANDY: Something has happened and they're going to take you away!

(She looks down at their entwined hands, becomes scared.)

MANDY: I can't feel your hand.

MIKE: It's there.

MANDY: You can do anything. Don't ever let anyone stop you.

MIKE: Okay.

MANDY. I'm a bad mother.

MIKE: You're not.

MANDY: And you're lying! Don't you see? If you lie, no one will know you, how beautiful you are. And you can't trust their love until they do. *(pause)* You shouldn't be here.

(She lets go of his hand.)

MIKE: But I want to be with you.

(Piano version of "Jake and Evelyn" from Chinatown creeps in.)

MANDY: Close the curtains. People will forget about us. We'll be born into something else. Radiant creatures without history. Won't that be fun?

(Pool lights shimmer around her, and she almost disappears in them as they slowly fade, and he watches, not knowing what will happen. Music continues.)

PART FOUR

Scene 13

(Lights up on Audrey. She stands and holds a rusted refrigerator door handle. Her eyes are closed. Mike enters and goes to her. Her Day of the Dead make-up is smeared. Music fades.)

MIKE: This isn't a good place to sleep. It's cold.

(She opens her eyes.)

AUDREY: It's a refrigerator.

MIKE: Where's the house to go with it?

AUDREY: Erosion.

MIKE: I don't see any food. I'm taking you home.

AUDREY: This is my home.

(Pause.)

MIKE: Who are you?

AUDREY: A girl.

MIKE: I don't see a girl's bed. What are those things with the curtains called?

AUDREY: Canopy beds.

MIKE: Or any dolls.

AUDREY: I'm too old for those. I've gotten older, even though I don't look it.

MIKE: Like a vampire.

AUDREY: I used to hear my mother calling, but then it stopped.

MIKE: I bet she never gave up.

AUDREY: She had another child. I have a sister now. They moved away.

MIKE: Did somebody hurt you?

AUDREY: For a little bit.

MIKE: And then what happened?

AUDREY: I was put here.

MIKE: Is anyone else here? I feel things, eyes watching maybe.

AUDREY: There were other children.

MIKE: Let's get them.

AUDREY: They're gone.

(She steps out, looks.)

AUDREY: There's someone out there.

(He looks.)

MIKE: It's a fire. It'll be warm, you need to get warm.

(She looks at his arm.)

AUDREY: You burned yourself once, a long time ago.

(He doesn't answer, he's thinking.)

AUDREY: How did it happen?

MIKE: I don't recall.

(A beat of eye contact; she starts to go toward the fire.)

MIKE: Wait.

(Mike catches up to her.)

MIKE: What's your name?

AUDREY: You never knew that.

MIKE: Where are you from?!

AUDREY: Fontana.

MIKE: Who are you?!

(Her grabs her arm, her demeanor changes, she becomes scared.)

AUDREY: I don't want to!

(He lets her go.)

MIKE: I'm sorry, I didn't mean. . .I just want to help you.

AUDREY: Like before?

(He stares at her, remembering something.)

MIKE: The girl in the field. . .

AUDREY: *(looks off)* The man who scares you. He's coming.

Scene 14

(Boozoo Bajou's "Rainy Night in Georgia" plays. Jesus enters with a piece of paper with a painted fire on it stuck to a piece of wood, he places it onstage and exits. A stick with a raw hot dog in a bun pokes out from the offstage. The branch wiggles around. Carpy enters, he is holding the branch. He dances around with the weenie in his own idiosyncratic way and ends up near the fire. Audrey and Mike approach him. Song fades.)

CARPY: Want a weenie, little girl?

(She takes it off the stick. As she does, a transformation comes over Carpy and he is feeble. Audrey runs off.)

CARPY: Well then, that's settled!

(He approaches Mike, he now needs the stick to walk.)

CARPY: Do you know about the history of this house? All bad. Crickety clack. . .if you're not careful you can fall through the floor boards. You could keep falling, who knows. You've seen the end of "The Man Who Would Be King," right? *(pause)* A devil cult was here in the 70s. Some teeth from 100 years ago are there in a corner. If only they could talk, crickety clack. An old oil lamp, a broken champagne glass, pig bones. Scrap from history. I found a hooker's old diary. In the hall there's peeling red and gold wallpaper; this was a bordello that serviced hog men. But Mulholland stopped by here, and the Rat Pack too on their way to bullshit Palm Springs. They screwed here but thought they were too good to live in the Inland Empire. A place that's out of time and quaint and greasy. I was whizzing east on the 10 one day and I thought, something's out there. . .

MIKE: This is the house where the killer took the children.

CARPY: Now, now, calm down. That wasn't me. I'm just squattin'. There's some kind of bed in a wall that still works over there.

MIKE: It was vacant when I was a kid.

CARPY: Did you bring girls here to make out?

MIKE: No.

CARPY: Well that was dumb. There's something romantic about a lone Victorian that slipped through the cracks of the demolition list. How about a smore?

MIKE: No thanks.

CARPY: Don't got any anyway. Can you help me sit by the fire, then?

(Reluctantly, Mike helps Carpy sit.)

CARPY: Join me 'cause I'm not gonna stare up at you like the jolly green giant.

(Mike sits. An orange glow encompasses them. Outdoor noises.)

CARPY: I like the stars. But we seem to be alone. Hey, isn't that what's his name's belt? I always thought recognizing constellations would get me laid. It hasn't. Well, welcome back to Fontana, or Felony Flats as some of us call it. Ever get the feeling they've left us behind on the far edge of the LA galaxy, with the snakes to breed, rusting moon towers, outlaw motorcycle gangs.

MIKE: The Hell's Angels started in Fontana, in 1946.

CARPY: Do you ride?

MIKE: No.

CARPY: A Chinese girl I tried to screw had a mo-
ped. She had little feet that fit into those little ped-
als, and probably a little pussy. Oh well. Pass me
those beans.

*(Mike passes him a nearby can with a spoon sticking
out of it.)*

CARPY: Food always tastes better by a fire, don't it?
I wish I had some bacon but I don't eat pigs anymore. Couldn't get those slaughter screams out of
my head. . .Fontana Farms was just down that dirt
road. It was the largest kill house in the whole
world. One hot summer a brain disease infected
the pigs and they had to shoot them all. The men
who handled the brains got sick. When they went
home to their families they didn't know them anymore. They didn't know who they were killing.

*(Mike looks to where Carpy was gesturing, Carpy
looks at him.)*

CARPY: I heard you were sent away. Where did you
go?

(Pause, Mike doesn't want to answer.)

MIKE: How did you meet my mother?

CARPY: I handled some investments for her. Just kidding. You were a cute little boy. I had a little crush on you. I mean. Over the years when you'd pop into my head I sometimes fancied myself your father.

MIKE: My father?

CARPY: Over the years. . .I thought things might change for me. I'd settle down with a woman, pass my goddamn genes on and have a family. Hemophilia runs in mine, how about you? Could you rub my feet a little? Please?

(Carpy takes off his shoe and lays his leg across Mike's. Mike reluctantly touches his foot.)

CARPY: They're clean feet, you don't have to worry. Ever since something happened to me I keep 'em squeaky that way. . .after the war. In New York. I was a young man and I found myself in a movie theater in the afternoon, a dark place where I could sleep off a hangover from a night with a wild nurse. Well I got as comfortable as I could in that shitty little seat, hoisted my legs on the seat in front of me, fell asleep a crumpled heap. Woke up sometime during the double Rita Hayworth bill and there was a guy sitting in the chair in front of me. He had taken off my shoes and he had his face buried in my feet. And his arm was moving up and down because he was whacking off. Is that the scariest story you've ever heard? I got more. *(pause)* He gave me a 20, anyway. So, I always keep 'em clean now. Wouldn't you? *(pause)* Hey, no offense but you're a terrible massager. You think a few pinches and squeezes does the trick? I hope you're not that kind of lover.

(Beat, fear flutters across his face.) I still hear your scream, across the dust. And then you went quiet as a snowflake or a stranger, and that was just as bad. *(pause)* Why she picked me I'll never know. Maybe it was the darkest of her nights I happened to come upon. I'd like to think there was something in me, something in my gnarled face that said, it's okay. . .I'll tell you this. Watching someone die. You see life. Shimmering, as it disappears before you. It's so beautiful.

(Mike takes a pocket knife out and holds it to Carpy's throat.)

MIKE: Did you kill her?

CARPY: Now why would I do that?

MIKE: Because you're a killer.

CARPY: I'm not. At least not here in Fontana. But I didn't kill your mother. Maybe you wish that I did.

(Pause.)

MIKE: What were you doing there?

CARPY: I was there to fuck.

MIKE: Did you love her?

CARPY: No. Do you love everyone you fuck?

(Pause.)

CARPY: It's funny. She was the one I was carnal with. But I can't conjure her face, much as I try. It's you I remember. In your pajamas with the little rockets on 'em. Luminous eyes. Looking up at me as I came out of her room.

(Pause. Mike takes the knife away.)

CARPY: I hoped that you hadn't forgotten me. Even if I became some sort of monster to you.

MIKE: I remember you.

CARPY: That's all I wanted. So someone knows I
was here. *(pause)* I wish I had made you a sand-
wich or something. What happened after I left?

(Pause, Mike lets himself remember.)

MIKE: The owl was out. I went to the window to see
him hunt, he liked to wait for rats to come to the
pool to drink. But I could only hear him, the moon
was too bright, it shined at me, stunned my sight.
The door was open to my mother's room. I went
to make some tea, she liked that, when she had a
black mood. I brought it in to her. I put her fingers
around the cup but it slid from the blood and
spilled and I burnt my arm on the hot liquid. It
hurt, and I screamed. Then I laid down on the bed
and closed my eyes. And it was like she was just
asleep. Next to me. . .

*(Mike has realized his mother killed herself and Car-
py was not her murderer.)*

CARPY: She looked at me and smiled like an angel,
before she cut into herself. And I think I did love
her, in the moment.

(Carpy stands, takes note of his surroundings.)

CARPY: There's a skeleton in a room back there with a ruffled dress on, one of the Gold Rush hookers. And then later, the dead children. Guess we're standing in the remains of a murder house, then. Every town has one. In which doors are axes, and boys and girls get baked into witch's treats.

(He steps out.)

CARPY: But I bet this was some whorehouse in the day!

(Happy, he falls to the ground, suddenly dead. Mike bends down to him and puts his hand on him.)

MIKE: Goodbye, Mr. Carpy.

("The Giggler" by Pat and the Wildcats plays. Jesus brings the liquor cart in. A finger falls off him as he exits. Mike puts it in his pocket. Slow fade.)

Scene 15

("The Giggler" morphs into Mandy singing Frank Sinatra's "In the Wee Small Hours of the Morning." Pool lights up. Mandy is singing, as if she is alone. She is in a 1950s house dress. Blood trickles down both wrists. Mike watches her and she becomes aware of him.)

MANDY: You don't live here anymore.

(She goes toward the pool lights.)

MIKE: Don't, it's dirty.

(She stops.)

MIKE: There are drowned rats in it.

MANDY: *(turns to him)* You were afraid of the water, but I held you and there were orange trees all around. Do you remember?

(Pause.)

MIKE: I tried to stay here with you. Find food for myself. But somebody smelled something rotting and they took me away.

79

(She is aware the rotting smell was her.)

MANDY: A child living alone is a bad thing.

MIKE: I killed an opossum. I cooked it on a stick in the yard. I was doing okay.

MANDY: No, it wasn't right. And not all meat tastes like chicken.

(She looks at him as if knowing they don't have long together.)

MANDY: You turned out so handsome.

(Pause.)

MANDY: Are you okay?

MIKE: I don't know.

(Beat, as she wanders out.)

MANDY: I stayed in this house. This town. I never thought to leave. When my father brought us here I was afraid, living at the base of a mountain. I thought there would be avalanches, rocks roaring through the house. It never happened, but we weren't safe. My mother broke him. Humiliated him at dinner parties, slept with other men. He still loved her, though. That love killed him. He was the only person I ever loved. Until you.

MIKE: Who was my father?

MANDY: Fathers are in dreams.

(She wanders away.)

MIKE: How could you do it?

(Pause.)

MIKE: If you loved me?

(She grapples with an answer.)

MIKE: If there were good things. About you. About us. I can't see or feel them.

MANDY: They're here.

MIKE: I hate you.

MANDY: That's okay.

(She smiles at him but there are tears in her eyes. She turns toward the lights.)

MANDY: A skeleton walks into a bar.

(He watches her.)

MIKE: I just.

(Mike takes a step toward her but that's all he is able to do. He is starting to feel feelings he hasn't felt in a long time, this is difficult for him.)

MANDY: The bartender asks what'll you have.

MIKE: Want more time. . .

MANDY: And the skeleton says I'll have a beer. And a mop.

(Jesus enters as Mandy steps into the pool lights and they shimmer around her. Jesus and Mike watch.)

MIKE: That's all I ever wanted.

(Lights darken on her.)

JESUS: It wouldn't be death then.

(Jesus exits. Mike feels the absence of people.)

MIKE: Momma - ?

(Mike stares where the pool lights and Mandy were.)

MIKE: I'm forgetting your face. How can I love you
  if I can't remember you? I'm afraid. . .

*("Gas Food Lodging main title" by J Mascis starts.
As lights slowly fade Mike starts to break down.)*

Scene 16

(Lights up on Mike, laying on the ground. Audrey sits near him, as before. He awakens, they have a beat of eye contact as song fades.)

MIKE: It was you I saw, in the field. When I was a boy. A man was taking you away and I couldn't. . .I'm so sorry.

AUDREY: It's what happened to me.

MIKE: I wanted to help you.

AUDREY: You couldn't have.

MIKE: *(scared)* I saw the killer. But I never saw his face.

AUDREY: His nose was red and he had candy.

MIKE: And I saw you again. At night once, behind our house. What were you doing?

(Pause.)

MIKE: You were looking in at me.

AUDREY: You were sad.

(Pause.)

MIKE: And Carla?

(She lets him continue.)

MIKE: You're not her daughter, are you?

AUDREY: That's what she sees when she looks at me. *(Looks off.)*

MIKE: Where will you go now?

AUDREY: Dead orchards, initiations for scarecrows.

MIKE: Why aren't you with the others?

(Beat, she looks off.)

AUDREY: Indians used to fish here, in the San Gabriel River.
The water was clean, and the men stood in it with spears while the women bathed in the sunlight. You might not know that when you look at it now. Dirty, full of trash. That's how it was.

("Hot Dreams remix" starts. She wanders to the tree. Lights flicker on her and the tree. Her limbs almost resemble part of it. He tenderly touches her cheek as lights fade.)

Scene 17

(Song plays in the dark for a beat. Colored lights start to flit across the stage around Mike, Audrey is gone from the tree. The Day of the Dead Festival is starting. Audrey enters, she carries a painted skeleton shaker. She dances around Mike and exits. Mandy and Carpy enter. Mandy now wears a wedding veil. A smiling skull mask is over her face, and one is over Carpy's too. He wears a wide brimmed hat and a rose is in his lapel. A cigar hangs out of his mask mouth. They link arms and walk toward the audience. They dance together around the stage and twirl off, in opposite directions. Jesus enters. He holds a child's umbrella that is upturned. He wears a blazer and only has one arm now. He moves in a way as if to avoid a strong wind blowing. He stands next to Mike. They look out. Song fades.)

JESUS: When you see where you used to live, it's like a dream, isn't it?

(Pause.)

JESUS: If you drive into LA at night, it's like a Shangri-la on the edge of a desert. We've all gone there in search of vagina, money, and fame. When you find this dream to be bullshit, you come here, to the Inland Empire!

(Jesus feels something coming. He takes a toy camera out of his pocket and hands it to Mike.)

JESUS: Shit, I forgot to give this to you.

MIKE: What's this for?

JESUS: Take pictures of everyone! Because we'll all be gone!

(Mike takes a picture of Jesus as wind builds. Mike gets the finger from his pocket and tries to hand it to Jesus.)

MIKE: Wait!

(Jesus gets blown around more.)

JESUS: Have you ever made a porno of yourself? Try to watch it, there's no horror worse. Well, I have to get to a nitrous party!

(Jesus spins around - Mike has to get out of his way - and exits. "Over" by Alpha starts. Mike is drawn to where he and Jesus were looking before, and steps towards it, as if with a purpose. Slow fade.)

Scene 18

(Lights up on Mike. He stands amongst scant detritus from a home. Some takeout menus are strewn about, and a small piece of stucco wall with graffiti is on-stage, as is part of a broken couch. He recognizes a dirty stuffed rabbit and picks it up. Song fades.)

MIKE: Mr. Bun. Have you really been waiting?

(Seeing it has an effect on him. He picks up an old menu and looks it over. Mandy enters, and stands, looking out. He sees her, she doesn't notice him.)

MIKE: My mother's silhouette at the window, star-ing out at a comb of galaxies. Is it a dream I am spinning? *(pause)* The rooms where we once lived; which room is my father? Would he have sat here, *(goes to the couch)* a face of shadows flickering so I can never know him? And then he hears the click of heels, and she leads him to her bedroom. . .

(Lights darken on Mandy as Mike is drawn toward the offstage/bedroom. He leaves Mr. Bun on the couch. Lights brighten past where Mandy was, to show Carla in her kitchen.)

MIKE: But it's only rooms. And we all have old houses we try to get back to. Maybe if we can, the people we loved will be there.

(He turns back to where Mandy was but she is gone. He sees Carla.)

MIKE: Did you find who you were looking for, at the festival?

(A wave of sadness comes over her. She doesn't answer. He goes to her. He knows her daughter was one of the murdered children.)

MIKE: What was your daughter's name?

(She turns to him as if he can give her an answer but knows he can't.)

CARLA: Is it something we did? The parents of this town?

(Pause.)

CARLA: He came out of the night, that's what they said. . .they found her in that house, with the others. Out in the field, where it smells of sage, and the town shimmers behind in the sun like a watercolor. She loved it there. I leave flowers for her.

(He doesn't know how to respond. He tries to touch her but she backs away, it's too difficult for her. She sees the menu in his hand.)

MIKE: Check out this old menu.

(She looks at it.)

CARLA: Hamburger, 50 cents. Coffee, a nickle. Little Bee's Diner. I've never heard of this place. Where did you find it?

(He moves toward something.)

MIKE: This was my window. I could look out at the pool.

(Carla is surprised, realizes he lived in this house.)

CARLA: I went to a skateboard party here after the water dried up. It was a meth house for a while. Then a gang took it over, the Diablo Locos, I think. After some years someone cleaned it up, took out the pool, put it up for rent. We moved in.

(Pause.)

CARLA: This was Pauline's room. My daughter.

MIKE: I could see the flowered wallpaper from the yard.

(She gets prickly.)

CARLA: I didn't change it. I don't want -

MIKE: It's okay.

(She realizes they're connected, through the house, through loss, now.)

CARLA: Welcome back.

MIKE: Thanks. But it's your house now. And then it will be someone else's, and years from now, maybe this place will all be underwater again.

(Mandy enters in the dilapidated part of the house. No one can see her. She looks out.)

CARLA: What do you want on your burger?

(He smiles at her.)

MIKE: Do you have any Thousand Island?

(She starts to fix it. Mike looks up.)

MIKE: We could see the stars.

CARLA: Right. No roof. . .

("Ce Matin La" by Air starts. They have a moment, there is lots to ponder. Carla goes back to preparing the food and he enjoys watching her. Mandy remains in her part of the house, alone. Tableau remains until lights fade. The end.)

More Great Plays From
Original Works Publishing

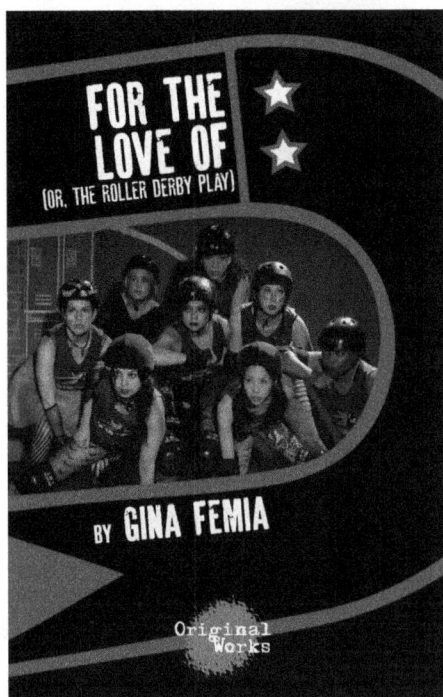

FOR THE LOVE OF by Gina Femia

Synopsis: When Joy gets on the Brooklyn Scallywags and meets the star, Lizzie Lightning, she and her long term partner Michelle find their lives turned upside down. *For The Love Of* asks how much you're willing to sacrifice – or lose – in order to follow your heart.

Cast Size: 9 Diverse Females

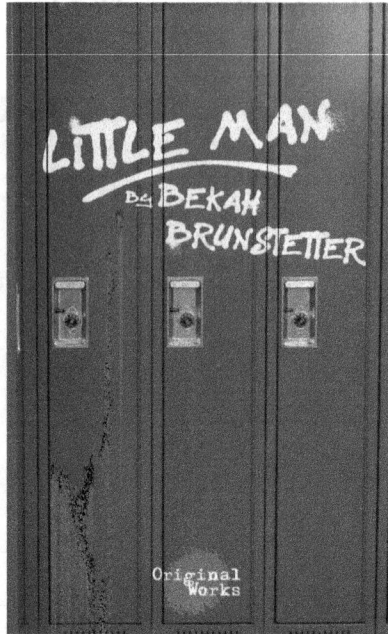

LITTLE MAN by Bekah Brunstetter

Synopsis: Howie has spent the last decade trying to forget the traumas of high school. But when an invitation to his ten year reunion arrives, he hops on a plane home to discover just what happened to the jocks, the prom queens, and the social outcasts- and whether anyone cares that he's a millionaire now. With wry wit and penetrating insight, Bekah Brunstetter's heartbreaking comedy takes us on a hilariously awkward and unexpectedly moving journey in which no one can completely abandon who they used to be.

Cast Size: 3 Males, 3 Females

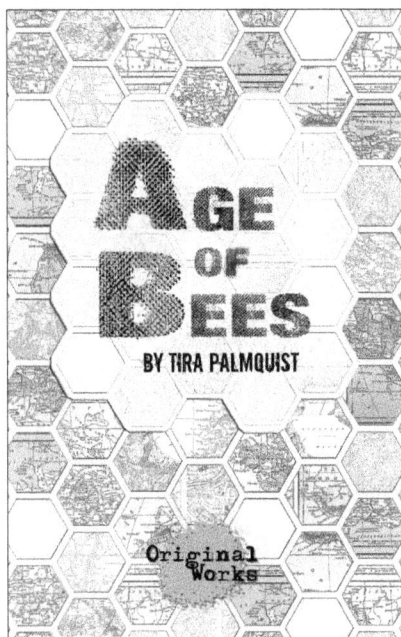

AGE OF BEES by Tira Palmquist

Synopsis: The bees have gone, disease and scarcity are rampant, but Mel, a young pollinator, finds refuge on an isolated farm. This place is fertile and safe, and Mel counts herself lucky to have a place where – even if it is not exactly happy – she has a purpose. When that purpose and safety are threatened, Mel faces an awful choice: will she risk leaving this relative safety, or will she hide from greater dangers, even if it means giving up some chance that something good can grow in this ruined world?

Cast Size: 1 Male, 3 Females

NURTURE by Johnna Adams

Synopsis: Doug and Cheryl are horrible single parents drawn together by their equally horrible daughters. The star-crossed parental units' journey from first meeting to first date, to first time, to first joint parent-teacher meeting, to proposal and more. They attempt to form a modern nuclear family while living in perpetual fear of the fruit of their loins and someone abducting young girls in their town.

Cast Size: 1 Male, 1 Female

NOTES

NOTES

NOTES

www.ingramcontent.com/pod-product-compliance
Lightning Source LLC
Chambersburg PA
CBHW062009040426
42447CB00010B/1981